CARAPACE

For Adele,

CARAPACE

Laura Lush

*– who made cunt
laugh so much
Laura
xo*

Palimpsest Press
5 King St, Kingsville, Ontario, Canada N9Y 1H9
www.palimpsestpress.ca

Book and cover design by Dawn Kresan. Typeset in Adobe Gara-
mond Pro, and printed offset on Rolland Zephyr Laid at Coach
House Printing in Ontario, Canada. Edited by Carmine Starnino.

Library and Archives Canada Cataloguing in Publication

Lush, Laura
        Carapace / Laura Lush.

Poems.
ISBN 978-1-926794-06-8

        I. Title.
        PS8573.U74C37 2011
        C811'.54   C2011-902027-0

We thank the Canada Council for the Arts and the Ontario Arts
Council for their support of our publishing program.

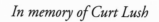

In memory of Curt Lush

CONTENTS

1

The Lake
Sunset
Autumnal
Swan
Marbles
On Your Birthday
Birthday Poem
Jackdaw
Time Under
Trek
Arctic Dream
Fox

2

Firstborn
Fish
Dog Story
Little Bird
Nursery Rhyme
Carapace
Mother
Birth
Baby
Captive
Eight Months
Right Now at This Moment
Five Thirty
Little Boy

3
Where He is Now
Day in, Out
The Deer
Highway
Destination
Portrait
Monster
The Fly
The Killing
The Beach
Bonespot
Hammock
Meditations
What the Eye Covets
March
May
On Becoming
The Ends of the Earth
Turtle
Downlight
Storm I
Storm II
After Storm

4
Love Story
Amaryllis
Some August Night
Stars
Phlox
Sheaf
Flowers
River
Glyphs
Samaritan

Night
Pond
Small Story
Tomorrow
Cosmos

Acknowledgments
Author Biography

1

THE LAKE

Quick. Get up. Maybe we can be happy again.
Light by light will turn on, dark lake no more.

Just these fat Buddha berries tumbling into our hands.
Summer again. Lazy grace of sun, lean banana warmth

grazing our backs. Fraternity of siblings face down
on the dock. Bronco barrels heaving under us—

gulp of deep dock water. Alive everywhere—the stutter
of water spiders, the squish of wogs through our fingers.

No parents about, just the nappy-winged aphids fussing
the air. Across the lake, a Sea Flea skip-slaps,

while the giant voices of the cottage people
splash in and out of our ears.

This is our childhood. Big lake buffeting us.
Suddenly naked, our bathing suits bobbing in brilliant colours,

one towel between the three of us.
Who will be the first to snap it up?

Quick hand-scoop of your blue trunks
as you scrabble to the highest rock.

Ha Ha King of the Castle. Dirty rotten bummed rascals.
Tiptoed on cliff's edge, we watch you. Hands stretching up,

fingers steeple-pose. Arch back once. And jump.
No time for clouds to call. Shock of water-split.

Are you gone? For days, we wait, follow the sound
of lake rings where a stone or some lost thing touched.

Our beautiful *Loch ness*. Twist of loon-neck rising.
Beak to surface, then down again. *Laughing. Laughing.*

SUNSET

I turned to pick up a shell.
You were standing on the beach,
grown out of this sand, our father-totem.
Wind divots whirled your ankles. They could
have easily lifted you, if not for your eyes,
anchored to the lake's skyline, gazed the vastness,
our churlish splashing, might of bullish waves.
And when we looked back, you were suddenly in.
Water shoaling your thinned body, the
translucent shine of your skin through the dark
of the lake. And as your hands dipped the water,
brought them to your face, I knew this was your
bit for us. Then we walked back to our blanket,
toweled our bodies, waited for the sun to shuttle down.

AUTUMNAL

Like Attis and Adonis, you left in October.
Blaze of orange leaves, shiver of birds wavering
on the telephone lines. Where else to go?
You left no tracks, no sign *Gone for Lunch.*
Be back in ten minutes. Only the sky, intemperate,
knows for sure. What life unspools.
　　　　Floating for years, adrift, banged-up
raft hitting reef after reef. Should we look
for you in spring? Some crow flaunting
black on black. Surely not in summer with
its lovers that think they will live forever.
Autumnal. The way the trees sough.

SWAN

If this swan suddenly lifted.
Really lifted and disappeared
over the blue of the pond,
would you come back again?
Would you step into us,
even for a breath-second?
So we would cry no more.
So we could let you die right
this time. Not alone breaking
into that night. But bird-taken,
quiet. Sweep of wing
lifting you.

MARBLES

I found them in your room
tucked in the same blue velvet
Crown Royal bag, the gold rope of the cord
still securing your childhood.
I assure you, I opened the bag as if it were
holding all the secrets of your Paleolithic world.
And the marbles rolled out—
each smooth round noise.
Small glass pommels
kept inside so long, barely remembering
your ten-year-old hands sizing them up.
How your own brown eye would squint down—
your perfect pale blue ball, lighting gold
running through it, its pain line
staying with you all your forty-four years.
Let me hold you, blue marble.
Let me warm you, finally.

ON YOUR BIRTHDAY

As I am walking to Sobeys to buy your birthday cake—the drifts
higher than this city has seen for a long time—sun on this irrepressibly

sunny day, I think of how much you hated birthdays,
the light shining on you. Imagine what you would be doing now

had you decided to stay. Do you see the way we walk outside
of ourselves, our spirits gutted in the trees, the wild wing-throttle

of our thoughts—this *never again*—flabbergast and spent?
This is our living. Come, take a look at the world through

our eyes. Its endless circling, axle's anguished spinning. These lit
candles—the faltering of our breaths as we try to wish you back.

BIRTHDAY POEM

Why oh why the cup
on the counter,
the lazy way the spoon
leans toward me.

Don't tell me the wind blazing
through the window
will change everything.

The cup falls, the spoon
reluctantly unmoors.
The whole world in
its porcelain sides.

That's when I realize
that at 45, I have already
outlived you.

JACKDAW

Hooded daw teetering above the tree-line,
      you swooped down, took him
with you that night. Saw him chancing on you.
      Thin-legged, balancing on a tightrope
of wind. *I know you have him.* Coveted in underwing—
      slate of grey. He's in your dark maw,
your clattering rook. Give him back to our day,
      no place in the riff of your song,
the raw tin of your *chyak-chyak*, taunting.

TIME UNDER

How ordinary it all is. The world knowing
nothing else. *Being born, dying.* The bereft's only trick—
to die *and* live, the desert and bones of day-to-day.
No plan, no escape. The colossal effort of one foot in front
of the other. What gifts! Life without the sentient. No music,
no colours, no way of feeling the rubbed out spaces
where we once breathed. Grief, a leg up for a very
long time. Until boredom unstalls, drifts its dark
balloon into some other's unprepared room.

TREK

We walk for miles. God-planned whiteness.
Scats of ice, wolves bunched like scarves.
The wind forcing cruelly.
We are nothing but our own salvation.
Waterless and dark. Our souls are leaving.
Blaze of sun and pink. We rise, sticks in hand,
walk toward the mercy of any god.

ARCTIC DREAM

Snow-swaddled body flanked by flags,
sun-charred laugh, the barely-stitched-together

wind. Then the single tusk of a narwhal
surfacing, a ship dynamited free from its winter

grave. Its sleek hull bludgeoning ice floe
after ice floe. Huddled in night fortresses,

numb to the grieving of snow dogs. Sometimes
a noise rises from the depth of tundra—

neither animal nor human. A sound like the chewing
of carrion, the spit-back of bones twitching

the night air. It is saying he will come back,
swell like the din of a thousand drums beating

the Arctic into deafened ears.

FOX

When the fox died,
the whole forest died.
What was it about the fox?
Clever, for sure; wit enough
to hole all of his body in dirt.
Every now and then, that tail—
spuriously red, flashing through trees.
Damn pretty shame
of it all.

2

FIRST BORN

My brother came first, the one who had to brave the distance
between the farmhouse and the end of the laneway
each morning. The one who had to defend my sister and me
when we pelted cars with snowballs, knock down the paperboy
for stealing my wallet. Go to Cubs, learn to light fires,
protect my mother from door-to-door-salesmen.
Hold a hockey stick even though he didn't want to.
Shake hands with uncles, admire their wide-belled ties.
Learn to drive, squeal tires, walk the dog,
Chase it back home again. Had to swallow the worst
of the family traits. Like a snake swallowing frogs.
Had to do everything first. And right.
Walk that long lane alone. One foot in front of the other,
wolves nipping at his heels.

FISH

Upstairs, your room
bubbled quiet.
In the tanks, the small
private world of gills.
Water the colour of underworld.

Sometimes a tetra
beaming its blue fin at me.
An angel-fish, sanctimonious,
fluttering.

Each tank stirring
with a different life
As if knowing that you, too,
would be different one day.
Brave guppy swimming
with its clear silver belly.
A glove without a lining.

DOG STORY

His name was Robbie McLaughlin and he was our dog.
He was black and forlorn, and he drove my mother crazy.
He crawled on his belly from the yard to the kitchen
so he could be with her. He fell in love with her cats,
her skirt, her bone-white ankles. Then one day,
Robbie McLaughlin dragged his old-dog body down
to the end of the lane and waited, while my mother,
oblivious, sat in the kitchen and also waited.
Later, she was inconsolable.
Where was her Robbie McLaughlin now?
Where was that *rough beast?*
What heaven or hell
was he slouching towards now?

LITTLE BIRD

I heard a little bird the other day
and thought of you. It was the kind
of bird that sings briefly, then lifts.
Wings, the whole wide sky.
Neither happy nor sad. It just wanted
to let me know it was there. Much
like the way you had always been.
Lightness of bird hopping from
branch to branch. And then off
to your particular blue.

NURSERY RHYME

Shined up, glossy swag hewed
in night. The moon again. Marooned,
still as snake-eye. A hitherward light
barely shying the trees. We would give
anything to see you again. Sudden chuff
of wind. No more of stars. Their sharp
pixilated fall-away as lightning
sears the muscled flanks of earth.
Raw of red. Somewhere a sailor is singing.

CARAPACE

Some foetus or fiddlehead curled
to a fountainhead of flesh in shell.
Spine and ribs fused to scutes of bony plates.
Your buffer against stones and the bruised
keel of your back-to-front lifeline—your ridge
of chance. Cracks that fill in themselves.
Fill with bone. And heal.

MOTHER

Hands cupped under
the swell of her belly.
A pearl, hewn tight.
Such sadness shining her shut.
Look how it holds on.
Tiny unformed feet
kicking at her sides.
Even she doesn't know what
Makes life stay or go.

BIRTH

Like an arm suddenly unmuscled, the belly
now unsprung. Legs akimbo, as you are airlifted

with gloved hands from under the white hospital sheet.
You arrive with tufted hair, fingers red and old.

A nose that sniffs out milk. Are you some small alien
come to snatch my next 20 years? Or love that's finally

arrived with a yawing pink mouth? For three days,
we lie on the hospital bed as the masked nurses—

blip of SARS—swish open the curtain. Dare them
to be awed. Elsewhere, the hushed voices of the fathers,

their awkward offerings of flowers and candy. Tethered
tethered to the bed, the wives moan, bodies warred by birth.

Life, again. This old life somehow begetting you.
Let me know how you see all this. Later—

waking up with the sun in your mouth.
Let me know how you see all this.

BABY

Tell me all your secrets.
Why you sway from side to side.
Suck at your gherkin toes.
I am old and your mother.
You're the only one I haven't lost.
Would you fight for me?
Or run the way of some men?
Even a baby has the power
to drown another.
I would save you. That's a given.
Sacrifice or else.
Tell me what else is more
beautiful, more punishing
than milk?

CAPTIVE

There is no morning
other than the morning
I wake with you, hold
you as I did those long nine months.
Did I smile when I felt
you drum my stomach?
To tell the truth, you scared the hell
out of me. It was you who held me
captive then, made me list like a boat
from side to side,
the wash of your wet warm sac.
Okay, let's call it even.
both of us have been gatekeepers,
both of us have held this cold gold key.

EIGHT MONTHS

How I envy you.
Skin embossed with kisses,
milk in the mouth,
subitus burst on the tongue.
The nubs of your teeth
such sweet Braille.
So cry all your nights and days.
Cry because it's good. The lungs
new and tender. Know that I will
listen outside your door.
The Good Mother. The Good Mother.
So it goes. The push-pull of your blue-slate
eyes, the way my mouth trips a bit
when I say, "My son." Grip hard.
Hold on tight. We're off.

RIGHT NOW AT THIS MOMENT

I walk into your room,
the twitch of your hands
around your bottle.
This moment of succor
I will not take.

I could tell you all sorts of things—
but you are so very smell
and do not know the machinations
that will make up your world.
This *tableau vivant* all yours.

FIVE THIRTY

I have been up since 5:30. Sleep snatched by
the panic of cries from the other room, my son
untwisting from some dream. He wants milk, warmth—
the clench of my arms around him. His head lolls
against my shoulder as I carry him to my bed.
One day he will hate me. Just because I made
him the way of all boys. Tough and splendour
in his grit for life. He will also love me, but
a little less than now. Now is survival, the want
of my protection. But for now, he is my whole
garden. This son not to grow broken.

LITTLE BOY

Across the yard you fly, chasing the bees'
yellow noise. Snap and twig-break—
horn of Keryneia's hind gripped
between your hands.
With Herculean might, twists of foot,
gnash of heel into earth.
You are here. I watch from the deck,
a magazine fluttering in my hands.
Never mind these words. You are here,
and you love better than I.

3

WHERE HE IS NOW

In a Charles Addams cartoon—rascal of boy perfecting
his dark oddities over and over again. In Foghorn Legghorn's,
Ah say, Well Ah say now. In the doodles of scrawl on Big Chief
writing tablets. In the squat and humble of the hens and chicks.
In the posthumous blaze of the poppies. In my father's eyes,
the slow gait of his hound loping behind him. In my mother's opera,
her kitchen swelling with tenors. In my sister's paroxysms
of laughter, her familial impressions. In the Huck Finn of my son
racing along a riverbank. In his empire of kiltering boxes.
In the chuffed grin of a cat stretching supine on the sidewalk.
In the hollowed body of a fossil, the vivid green of a hummingbird,
its sinusoidal waves. In the crack of a book's spine, in the internal
breakings of a Tim Buckley song. In the *duende* of a Lorca poem,
its susurrations of suffering and sorrow. In the emotional geometry
of a shell. In a turtle scaling its glass walls, the gleam of its ascent.

DAY IN, OUT

Wolves once sung through
this night. And there is
no guessing the thunderstruck
way the jackrabbit was snared.

THE DEER

Buckling into the snow, bloodless breath
shorting from nostrils.
Such fear hanging from it.

Was this William Stafford's
deer-on-the-highway just seconds before?
Or did the quick-cocking of a gun
Triggering its bolt, horizon flatlining
Against the drifts of snow?

It broke into flight, shot past the sound
of my voice calling. What human hope
wanting to be gone of *it*,
far from its huntedness.

And months later, I knew I'd change
my mind when the deer's hollowed canoe
of ribs broke like twigs under
my own feet, running.

HIGHWAY

It's a road, broken. Scarred by car wrecks, deers bunting
into windshields—bits of lives scattered across.

Brute of a highway brooking soft shoulders.
I walk this road. Stop to unlodge a stone. It hurts.

The way nothing has ever hurt. So much of that road
nothing. Yet terror-capable. The very lay of it, bustling

with transports, the incomprehensible speed of life—
rabbits caught middle-frozen

on haunches, dithering this way and that.
Bulrushes—quiet and reed-necked, sluicing

the gutters. Fear, like the sky with its ribs out. But it just
goes on, flat, tarred—a whippet stretch of long

and black. Not even the sun, orange and fierce,
can tack this road down.

DESTINATION

Today, the ordinary look of a commuter mussed
    and bleary by early morning's
rise. Tucked in, shackled by shirt and tie.
    The tired lean of his body—the paucity
of his smile when I offer him my seat. Uneasy acceptance.
    Water-blued eyes. Emotions
no longer clandestine. Bare and thin as the train's
    metal peal across the tracks.

PORTRAIT

Something stolen and haunted. Around him,
billboards, placards, rusty iron. A grunge
that can only feed the spirit traumatized.
Never-ending night. He wakes to the sound
of his lungs, the girl still lodged in the frontal
lobe, the dopamine sucking at the memory
fossils. There is no need to say if he gets
back what he lost. All shows in that face—
still and frozen as if under a glass cloche.

MONSTER

How else to imagine you but dark and lonely?
Illusive beast. Uneasy stealth from light
and the human eye hungry for your surfacing.
Some prehistoric Bunya that can only glimpse
itself in another. Tragic lifeline. Trajectory
of the hunted. Catch you in a photograph.
Better yet, a souvenir—some rag of fur.
Anything to prove that your monster
suffers more than we.

FLY

On the night table, a fly, wings
derelict in sun. Still and succored
by afternoon heat. Then fly buzzes
in that fly way that makes me
want to lift my hand and kill.
But for its eyes—huge ocular mysteries,
tomed planets no longer in orbit.

THE KILLING

My 80-year-old father woke
to the sound of his two cross-hounds,
opened the summer kitchen door to
the noxious chomping of a full mother coon.
She was better than him. Had snuck in and ruined
her prehensile claws through the dog food. That's when
the hounds descended—jump-jawed on its neck and the
terror of *some* thing's death moments away. But my
father pulled them off. This one was his. Loaded his 12-gauge,
cocked the gun twice and shot. It was easy, and he gladly
cleaned the blood-spatter, the victory full in him. How many
other chances would he have to prove his protection
over us—asleep upstairs—the wheeze of our dreams
interrupted by such things? For morning, he would tell
his tale and we would listen to this man, our father.
The way this killing had to be.

THE BEACH

For a while, the kite full and blue
in the sky before it collapses onto the hard
brown beach. Flaps in tatters as children run
behind it, certain of lift and wind-surge, of again.
But the kite rues that endless sky, the string
that pulls and twists, bonsais its shape. The reel
of a bird as it descends on all that is open—
        the waves' histrionics—blustery, capped,
glad for the sun-lathered bodies that bob and jump.
Such slaps, froth up, down—throttle, faces
full of bottom-sand. Feeding on the gust
and throw of this beach.

BONESPOT

Broken down over the fence, the sun
          sets on the single bonespot
in the grass—jagged and picked,
          some dog's gnawed artifact
teethed and whittled, a small blood mote
          hardening. It is just
like the sun to be there again, flooding the sky's
          tether and stretch. Always lurking
in these hills, warred and roughed. Coming up
          quick—a moment's sly—a whale
surfacing, blowhole spewing. Whiff of sky,
          then back down again.

HAMMOCK

New moon, night hushed to grass swish.
     A star trick-falls and a hound
bites his way through the dark. Watch this man
     swing in a hammock—life spent
in the cool liminal pocket of air. Slow twists
     of willow branch wheezing out
his time. Night birds rush overhead. The sound of
     a zippered wind. Gust and heart-pound.
Tucked away—an arrhythmia of emotion. I won't tell
     you how easily it can stop. But for
the hammock. Ask that man. His swing secret.

MEDITATIONS

Melded together like small white stars
on a skillet of flat earth, frozen. And the
gilt-brightness of days and nights as
the shined eye of a mock moon
illuminates this naked canvas. Sometimes,
from afar, white moving on white—
lumbering of polar bear,
his big head searching up.

WHAT THE EYE COVETS

Sometimes it's a simple shell
loosened on the beach which
grabs—possesses instantly
as if some fossilized doppelganger
of reptilian brilliance is suddenly
shining itself back. The world making beauty—
until some wave smashes down.
What now the eye?
The heaviness of the small and lost
floating under lids.

MARCH

Underneath, grasses move—small itches swaying like Sargasso.
Jackdaws swoop and thieve what they can. Beaks like the long

curved nails of a sarcophagus' mummy. Light, then no light.
All the shine turned in. Sun coppered into the hard brown earth.

Breath of dog sniffing the last lick of bone. Shadow of rabbit—
shiver of white haunches. Sundown, a locomotive rumbling over

snowed branches. Percolating undergrowth—a burst of flowers,
green-horned, fierce. Nubs' toughened spikes. Ratcheting colour.

Sky blue tumbling over the cool thaw of ponds. The *ume* plum
swaddled in rice. Desire trapped, quiet as mustard seed.

Salacious lettuce chattering under the cold tap water. Chair in front
of window. Book in hand. Rose frozen into its red bleed.

Grifter. *Take and can.* Gunny sack over shoulder. Move on.
Mountain and flurry. Streams moving. Fish flipping on the banks—

pinked and alive.

MAY

In May, the flowers—beauty
rigged to stark-green stems.
The anthem of lone things.
Irises—petals crimped, yet a papery
lightness somehow extolling.
Grow tall. Bloom/Die. Do not leave us.
Shake of deep purple against
the cold steel of fences.
So this spring eye can reap
or spoil.

ON BECOMING

The animals with their unmoving eyes.
Guile of winter snow.

The reach of a mother's teeth—
Catastrophe averted. Proximity of prey.

Red-brown shifts of fox moving.

A field covers its bones. Trees die
Cored and naked. Hearts must fix themselves.

THE ENDS OF THE EARTH

Were I to go there, I would eat snow
for days, drift south from time to time—
freeze like sea ice, lay down my floes
for caribou to cross.
I would not waver, be no barrier.
Plunder my way down to the sea floor,
let fragments of myself fall
off, my human tabular finally free.

TURTLE

The glottal sound of the wind
as the turtle braces the bank, readies the climb
of her life. Some say ritual. Flips mud
in her ancientness. The almost
squawk of shell. Nothing here for her,
but the away sound of forest,
creatures slow-moving into night.

DOWNLIGHT

The door handle we rub for luck.
Some trick of wind that harasses our windows.
Nobody there. Just this thought that glints
in and out of memory. Your voice stopped in our ears.
Life shot blue in the veins.
Oh gather us. Dust motes whirling dead corners.
Heat-ghosts bumping. Our proclivity for lost.
Dirt in our faces. Kick in throat. The light finally down.

STORM I

There in the thick, middled in the tree
        between two peaks
of Ararat, a hurt-thing of little consequence
all but gone. Never completely knowing
what from what—the blustered fields,
the tossed dark of air.

STORM II

Without warning, it filleted the trees—broke the hard oaks and maples
       so the trunks mere wind-sticks batoning through the air.
Haunt of blue, the roughened lines of birds leaving the sky,
       no godly-thing about. The quiet suddenly
lost. And, yet, the storm *not* there. Footprints in dirt.
       Rabbits noosed by invisible lines. The ghost of hunters
retreating over hills. Cacophony of calls and the chilled air, butter
       shine of bullets. Mix of twigs breaking underfoot—the hard
thoughts of last night—a body curled into us—fug of room, filigree
       of soul we tore though before our feet took us
to the stretch of highway, that moose lifting to human-scent.
       Far from the trucks wheeling, the flicked-out cigarettes
tumbling from windows, their embers sparking dark pavement.

AFTER STORM

And then
a quiet so ordinary nobody
knew the better.
Sun everywhere—
sky-glad birds and trees big again,
posturing
their dark loud arms over the earth.

4

LOVE STORY

Romance of grit and water.
Leaves whorled around the blackened trees.
Sun on this bedrock—tooled
breathlessly into its final thin coil.
Some chancing upon, a goldening cry for life.

AMARYLLIS

On the chair, I sit as the amaryllis
stubbornly blooms. Orange as fire,
but not nearly as angry. For three days
it does not open. I taunt it with water, give
it front seating by the window, flick its dandy
of a tail as I walk by. *Fool.* Oh sure, it wants me
to look and fawn. I take the scissors,
snip dangerously close, skulk back to my corner,
tough and spiked up. But oh, when the times comes,
how I lean into that kiss.

SOME AUGUST NIGHT

So I lied. This *is* a love story. Crickets, fog, the crooked
lines of stars. No time, no dark rivers, no rapids.
Just the quick whip of a lizard's tail as dawn snaps up.
Dumb and loved-out, our own tectonic plates shifting
open. The soul out. Shock of *Too late.*
Shut it anyway. Then drive home. We just drive home.
The lie of our ghosted bodies in each other's beds.
The sheets still tangling. Our do-nothing of it all.

STARS

Inexorable quiet. Wind timing itself through
the long grasses. Shiver of light, some star extinguishing.
Night absolves. Like some monk shaking off
the earth. You need to get to me before my heart travels.
The moon is somewhere. Buried under all that wreck.

PHLOX

Look at the cloister of phlox.
Purple splashing the eastview
of hayfield, young and garrulous
with its fresh-yellowed bails.

Reverence aside, they are effervescent, fulfilled.
Or maybe it's just us. Gawking—
entranced by their steamy
blaze. Once or twice,
life like that, the circuitry of all-things-after
suddenly ruined, the lay of love always
slightly off balance.

Roots sinew through the toughest foundation—
grab and tighten.
A fizzled breath releases
and you turn the corner again.

SHEAF

Crows arresting
in black wings. Shackled, the trees
bend their massive fulcrums snapping
back as roots grip, then break
from underrocks. Bamboo click-thins
together, sounding their needs. The way
of your own want, grasp of hands,
a sheaf of grass so sharp
it cuts across your palm,
your own voice keening.

FLOWERS

The living chattel the earth.
      Everywhere
flowers offing their colours.
Theirs is no easy story. Rape of
pollen. Solipsism of bees. Propagation
unchecked. They'll see us through another
season. There's a field, close by, that doesn't
let go of its flowers.

RIVER

I've been down to the river
two and two hundred times.
Seen the ghosts of white lilies
floating over the heaviness
of stones. Wondered at the small
spools of eddies still sucking at the dead.
Not quite over, the flash of lives relive themselves
in one lustrous moment of sun. No ordinary
gospel played out on these banks. Bulrushes
prickling with the low voices of frogs.
I lean over the banks, splash
my face with these waters.
The rightness of this river.

GLYPHS

It takes forever to leave this earth—its mysterious
glyphs, its stubborn lichen, the smouldering embers

of man-tracks. All the long, shimmering shoals—
lit-up flowers flaming out of the toughened

loam of hill. The barely-alive roots' blackening sprawl—
wind's slow distraction across the valley before storm strikes.

A shunt so deep in our hearts. Yet somehow stumbling
toward happiness, head-on—smashed up, bumbling like stars.

SAMARITAN

I found a leaf the other day,
red and tattered on the sidewalk.
The wind kept lifting its
papery body every time
I tried to catch it.
I was trying to save it.
I had my reasons. None
of which were particular pure
or right.
But just human.

NIGHT

Moon sentry in Elizabethan glower.
Orchid knife of wind coring night. Flicks
stars out, one by one. Tiny sparks that ignite
at the touch of dark. Frogs blowing their croaks.

POND

Born out of it—
reeds tangled and bird
haunted. The grass in throes
of the sun. The rain's sorcery
of lines, whips of black.
Fantastic sheen of
pond rippling the frog
home.

SMALL STORY

So the tree. And the wrongful
way the wind de-leaved it.
Down to bare bark and skid-wracked
branches. But I'm exaggerating of course.
This is the law of all taking. Savour the small moments—
apples with their red out, skins glossed to luster.

TOMORROW

Incandescent, light-struck,
earth for another night.
Tell me how it will go.
The next few nights without stars.
Oh, but this is the mind's footwork.
Of course there will be stars.
Maybe not in this small sky,
But shining, always, somewhere.

COSMOS

Of the questions left:
Love, Death—this proxy of flower.
A shot-flew of petals
scattering fall—something
of the wind still mauls.
Why I take each day
on my way home from work—
stem snapping, break-point of heart.
My son saying, "Don't pick
the flower, Mommy."
I cannot help myself.
I need this purple, agape in mouth.
So all the world savages
such beauties.

ACKNOWLEDGEMENTS

First, thank you to Noelle Allen for passing this manuscript on to Dawn Kresan. As always, thanks to the Phoebe Walmer Collective (Sue Collins, Vivette Kady, Jim Nason, and Eddy Yanofsky) for all their support, great food, and laughs over the years; and finally, thanks to my late brother, Curt Lush, for lighting the fire of poetry in me, and for showing us how to live with compassion and humanity.

"Fox" appeared in Arc; "Cosmos," "Hammock," and "Glyphs" (formerly "Aleon") appeared in *Brick*. "The Deer" appeared in *The Malahat Review*, and "Amaryllis" and "Nursery Rhyme" appeared in *The Antigonish Review*. "Small Story," "Samaritan," "May," "After Storm," "Night," and "Flowers" appeared in *Canadian Notes & Queries*. An earlier version of "First Born" was first published in *Dandelion*. "Phlox" was included in the 2007 'Poem of the Week' series chosen by the 2006/07 Poet Laureate of Canada, John Steffler. "Marbles" first appeared in *Arc* and was also used as lyrics for a composition included in Austin composer Stephen Barber's *Astral Vinyl CD* (Navona Records, New Hampshire, 2011). Lyrics sung by metzo soprano Lucy Schaufer.

AUTHOR BIOGRAPHY

Laura Lush teaches academic English and creative writing in the School of Continuing Studies at the University of Toronto, where she is also completing her M.Ed degree. This is her fourth book of poetry. She has been widely published in anthologies including *The New Canon: An Anthology of Canadian Poetry* (Signal Editions, 2005), *Open Wide a Wilderness: Canadian Nature Poems* (Wilfred Laurier University Press, 2009), *The March Hare Anthology* (Breakwater Books, 2007), and *The Echoing Years: An Anthology of Poetry from Canada & Ireland* (Centre for Newfoundland & Labrador Studies School of Humanities Publications and Waterford Institute of Technology, Ireland). She has also published a book of short fiction, *Going to the Zoo*, Turnstone Press, 2002.